The Flag

OF OUR UNITED STATES

By James A. Moss

Colonel, United States Army, Retired
President General, The United States Flag Association

AUTHOR OF *The Flag of the United States: Its
History and Symbolism; The Spirit of the Amer-
ican Flag; The Flag of the United States: How To
Display It—How To Respect It; The American
Flag: Its Glory and Grandeur; Our Country's
Flag; etc.*

RAND McNALLY & COMPANY

CHICAGO

Printed in U. S. A.

Acknowledgment is made to Horydczak,
for the cover photograph, and to the
Standard Printing and Publishing Co.,
Huntington, West Virginia, for the use
of the illustrations on pp. 8 to 17, from
Flags of America, by Colonel William H.
Waldron—the best book the author
knows on this subject.

THE CONTENTS

WHAT THE FLAG MEANS

CHARLES EVANS HUGHES

This Flag means more than association and reward. It is the symbol of our national unity, our national endeavor, our national aspiration. It tells you of the struggle for independence, of union preserved, of liberty and union one and inseparable, of the sacrifices of brave men and women to whom the ideals and honor of this nation have been dearer than life.

It means America first; it means an undivided allegiance. It means America united, strong and efficient, equal to her tasks. It means that you cannot be saved by the valor and devotion of your ancestors; that to each generation comes its patriotic duty; and that upon your willingness to sacrifice and endure as those before you have sacrificed and endured rests the national hope.

It speaks of equal rights; of the inspiration of free institutions exemplified and vindicated; of liberty under law intelligently conceived and impartially administered.

There is not a thread in it but scorns self-indulgence, weakness, and rapacity. It is eloquent of our community interests, outweighing all divergencies of opinion, and of our common destiny.

(From a speech delivered in 1916.)

The original Star-Spangled Banner that flew over Fort McHenry during the bombardment on the night of September 13–14, 1814, and inspired Francis Scott Key to write our National Anthem (see p. 33). The Flag, 30 by 34 feet, is now in the Smithsonian Institution, Washington, D.C.

HISTORY OF THE FLAG

The flag of a people symbolizes their hopes and aspirations, their struggles and sacrifices, their joys and achievements. If these be fine and noble, their flag is great, but if their aspirations, conduct, and accomplishments be ignoble, then their flag means little or nothing. In other words, the flag of a country is what its people make it. It is nothing more, nothing less.

Those who founded this nation of ours, through their aspirations, struggles, sacrifices, and achievements, made and handed down to us a great country with a great Flag, symbolizing ideals and institutions which, in the short span of a century and a half, have made the United States a nation second to none in greatness and power, wealth and influence.

In order to understand properly the history of the Flag of the United States—its origin and evolution—it is necessary to know about the principal flags of other countries which have influenced its design. Especially should we be familiar with the development of the flag of Great Britain, which no doubt had greater influence on the design of the United States national emblem than any other flag.

THE FLAGS OF GREAT BRITAIN

CROSS OF ST. ANDREW

One of the earliest flags of Great Britain to have a possible influence on the Flag of the United States was the Cross of St. Andrew. From about the middle of the eighth century the Cross of St. Andrew, Scotland's patron saint, had been the national standard of that country. It was a white diagonal cross on a blue field (see p. 8), thus containing two of the colors of our present Flag. The Cross of St. Andrew was brought to America by the Scots during their early explora-

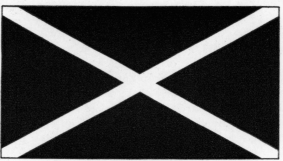

Cross of St. Andrew

tions and settlements in Nova Scotia at the time of the English settlements at Plymouth, Massachusetts, and Jamestown, Virginia.

Cross of St. George

CROSS OF ST. GEORGE

Another early flag of Great Britain of interest to us is the

Cross of St. George—a red cross on a white field. It was in the latter part of the thirteenth century that Edward I

Union Jack—The King's Colors

of England became so interested in the story of St. George and the dragon that he adopted the Cross of St. George as the flag of England (see p. 8). This flag was first unfurled

Meteor Flag—Red Ensign

in North America in 1497, by John Cabot, who probably landed on the coast of Newfoundland.

Union Jack—The King's Colors

In 1606, James VI of Scotland, who three years before had ascended the throne of England as James I, decreed that the Crosses of St. George and St. Andrew be united on one field (see p. 9) to typify the linking of the destinies of the two countries. The combination of these two Crosses brought together the colors of red, white, and blue, which almost two centuries later became our national colors. In time the new flag of James I became known as the Union Jack, the word "Jack" being derived from *Jacques*, the French word for James. The flag was also known as the Grand Union Flag and the King's Colors. It was the flag under which England colonized America and for a long time was used by the colonists. It flew from the mainmasts of the "Constant," which brought the English settlers to Jamestown in 1607, and of the "Mayflower," which brought the Pilgrims to Plymouth in 1620, while the Cross of St. George was displayed from the foremasts of these vessels.

Meteor Flag—Red Ensign

In 1707 a flag consisting of a red field* and the King's Colors as a canton was adopted as the national standard of Great Britain (see p. 9), and as such was well known to early American colonists. This Meteor Flag of England, as it was sometimes called, was also known as the British Red Ensign and continued to be the national flag of Great Britain until 1801. It was the flag of Great Britain in America throughout the War of the Revolution and the banner under which Cornwallis surrendered at Yorktown, October 19, 1781.

*A Glossary of Flag Terms may be found on p. 62.

Dutch Flags

While there is reason to believe that the British flags had the greatest influence in determining the design and colors of the Flag of the United States, it is probable that an influence was exerted also by the flags of the Dutch Republic, the United States of Netherlands, and the Dutch West India Company. For half a century before the English began colonizing the Middle Atlantic states, the Dutch had been settling and governing New Netherland, which consisted of the Dutch settlements in New York, New Jersey, Pennsylvania, and Delaware. So the Dutch flags with their dominant stripes and colors of red, white, and blue had been familiar to American colonists for over a hundred years. Incidentally, it may be noted that the word "stripe," so essential a part of our Flag vocabulary, is from the Dutch *strijpe*, "a stripe, streak."

Colonial Flags

Before the Continental Congress adopted a flag for the United States, in 1777, various banners of different designs were used in a number of the colonies. Those here mentioned were among the best known and most interesting.

Taunton Flag

In 1774, two years before the signing of the Declaration of Independence, the so-called Taunton Flag (see p. 12) was unfurled at Taunton, Massachusetts. It was, in reality, the Meteor Flag of England, with the word "Liberty" across the lower part of the red field.

Bedford Flag

The Bedford Flag, which waved over the "embattled

farmers" at Concord, April 19, 1775, when they fired "the shot heard round the world," is considered by many to

Taunton Flag

exceed all other Colonial flags both in interest and in historic value.

This famous standard is today carefully preserved in the

Bedford Flag

Public Library of Bedford, Massachusetts. A mailed arm extends from a cloud, the hand clasping a sword. A scroll

12

bears the motto, *Vince aut Morire* ("Conquer or Die").
The three disks are supposed to represent cannon balls

Moultrie Liberty Flag

(see p. 12). To this flag belongs the honor of being the first
flag of the American Revolution to receive a baptism of
British fire.

Bunker Hill Flag

MOULTRIE FLAG

This flag is said to have been the earliest displayed in the

13

South (1775). It was a blue flag with a white increscent in its upper right-hand corner. A year later the word "Liberty" was emblazoned on it (see p. 13).

The story of the Moultrie Flag's origin is interesting. When Colonel William Moultrie occupied Fort Johnson, on James Island, in September, 1775, his troops wore a blue uniform, with a silver increscent on the cap. Realizing that a flag was necessary, he improvised one having a blue field, with a white increscent in the canton. This was the flag that Sergeant Jasper so gallantly rescued on June 28, 1776, when the British fleet attacked Fort Sullivan at Charleston, South Carolina. For his gallantry the Governor presented him with his own sword and offered him a Lieutenant's commission, but the Sergeant, who could neither read nor write, declined the promotion, saying, "Sir, I am not fit to keep the company of officers."

PINE TREE FLAGS

Pine Tree Flags of different designs were very popular in New England, the pine tree symbolizing the hardiness of the New Englanders. One form, known as the Bunker Hill Flag, consisted of a blue flag with a white canton bearing the red Cross of St. George and a green pine tree (see p. 13). Another form of the Pine Tree Flag—the one adopted by Massachusetts in 1776—had a white field with a pine tree in the center, above which were the words, "An Appeal to Heaven" (see p. 16).

RATTLESNAKE FLAGS

Used especially in the South, the Rattlesnake Flag, in a variety of forms, rivaled in popularity the Pine Tree Flag. One form, known as the Gadsden Flag, had a yellow field with a coiled rattlesnake in the center, under which appeared the words, "Don't Tread on Me" (see p. 16).

Various reasons are given why the rattlesnake symbol should have been selected. Benjamin Franklin is said to have defended the symbol on several grounds: that the rattlesnake is found only in North America; that among the ancients serpents were considered possessed of wisdom and vigilance; that the rattlesnake does not attack without first giving warning; and that the number of rattles increases with age—hence the symbol was especially appropriate for the anticipated growth of the United States.

RHODE ISLAND FLAG

Because of the oft repeated claim that the design of the union of the Flag of the United States was suggested by the stars in the flag of Rhode Island, this flag is one of the most interesting of the Colonial flags. It had the word "Hope" in a white field, and thirteen white stars in a blue canton (see p. 17). The middle vertical and horizontal lines of three stars form the Cross of St. George, while the two diagonal lines of five stars form the Cross of St. Andrew, but whether this occurred through coincidence or design is not known.

FIRST FLAG OF THE UNITED COLONIES

Variously designated as the Cambridge Flag, the Grand Union Flag, or the Great Union Flag, the first flag of the United Colonies was flown over George Washington's headquarters at Cambridge, Massachusetts, January 1, 1776 (see p. 17). It had thirteen horizontal red and white stripes, with the combined Crosses of St. George and St. Andrew in a canton with a blue field (the King's Colors—see p. 9).

In fact, it was the Meteor Flag of England (see p. 9), with the solid red field divided by white ribbons so as to make

Pine Tree Flag

thirteen red and white stripes, representing the thirteen rebelling colonies. This similarity may at first seem strange, but it must be borne in mind that at the time the idea of

Gadsden Flag

independence from England was not seriously considered by the colonists, so that the King's Colors in this flag showed the allegiance which the colonies felt they still owed to the mother country.

Rhode Island Flag

When Washington heard, for the first time, the Declaration of Independence in New York City, July 9, 1776, the Grand Union Flag was flown for the occasion. While the

First Flag of the United Colonies

Army used this flag over barracks, camps, and fortifications, it never, so far as is known, carried it in battle. In fact, it

17

was short-lived, as it was naturally inappropriate and unpopular after the signing of the Declaration of Independence, July 4, 1776.

Adoption of Flag of the United States

On June 14, 1777, the Continental Congress in Philadelphia adopted the following resolution:

Resolved, That the Flag of the United States be thirteen stripes, alternate red and white; that the union be thirteen stars, white in a blue field representing a new constellation.

The significant part of this resolution is the words, "Thirteen stars, white in a blue field representing a new constellation," for it is in them that we find the very soul and spirit of the American Flag. These were the words which, like scintillating stars in the heavens, signaled to the world the birth of the first nation on earth dedicated to the personal and religious liberty of mankind.

It will be noted that the resolution of adoption did not prescribe how the stars were to be arranged. As a result, in the beginning they were arranged in various ways, including a circle. Some say the circle was to indicate the equality of the states, while others contend it was to symbolize the hope that the Union would be without end.

Two Stars and Two Stripes Added

In 1791, the state of Vermont was admitted into the Union, and in 1792, Kentucky was admitted. The representatives of these two states in Congress wanted their states recognized in the Flag; so on January 13, 1794, Congress enacted a law to the effect that, beginning May 1, 1795, there should be fifteen stars and fifteen stripes in the Flag (see p. 23).

1777 June 14. Saturday June 14 1777

— Resolved That the Flag of the united States be thirteen stripes alternate red and white that the Union be 13 stars white in a blue field representing a new constellation.—

The above is a facsimile of the original resolution passed by the Continental Congress, June 14, 1777, adopting the Flag of the United States. This was ten years before the adoption of the Constitution, September 17, 1787. The hand-writing is that of Charles Thomson, secretary of the Continental Congress.

Note that "Flag" is spelled with a capital *F*, but "United States" is spelled with a small *u* and a small *s*. Note, also, the wording, "the Flag of the United States," which gives us the correct, official designation of our national emblem.

In some Flags the stars were staggered in five horizontal rows of three stars each, while in other Flags they were arranged in three horizontal rows of five stars each, one directly above the other. The Flag that flew over Fort McHenry when Francis Scott Key was inspired to write "The Star-Spangled Banner" had its stars staggered in five rows (see p. 6).

Thirteen Stripes—Star for Each State

In 1818, the number of states having increased to twenty, Congress passed a law (1) giving representation in the Flag to the five states—Tennessee (1796), Ohio (1802), Louisiana (1812), Indiana (1816), and Mississippi (1817)—that had been admitted into the Union after the last Flag Act had been adopted, thereby increasing the number of stars to twenty, effective July 4, 1818; (2) returning the number of stripes to the original thirteen; and (3) decreeing that thereafter a star should be added to the blue field for each new state admitted into the Union, such addition to take effect on the Fourth of July following the date of admission into the Union—that is, the law provided, in effect, "Every Star a State; Every State a Star" (see pp. 60–61).

Stars Tell Growth of Nation

It is in the stars of the Flag that we read the growth of the American nation. As the nation has grown in size, so have the stars in the Flag increased in number.

At Beginning of Mexican War

From the time the stars increased to twenty, in 1818, to the beginning of the Mexican War in 1846, Illinois (1818),

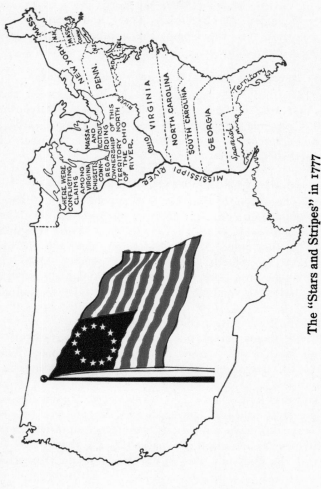

The map labels include:
HERE WERE CONFLICTING CLAIMS
VIRGINIA AND CONNECTICUT
MASSA-CHUSETTS AND CONNECTICUT REGARDING OWNERSHIP OF THIS TERRITORY NORTH OF THE OHIO RIVER.
NEW YORK
N.H.
MASS.
CONN.
PENN.
N.J.
MD.
DEL.
VA.
OHIO
VIRGINIA
NORTH CAROLINA
SOUTH CAROLINA
GEORGIA
Spanish Territory
MISSISSIPPI RIVER

The "Stars and Stripes" in 1777

In this early Flag the stars in the blue field were arranged in the form of a circle to signify the hope that the Union would be without end; also, to symbolize the equality of the states.

Alabama (1819), Maine (1820), Missouri (1821), Arkansas (1836), Michigan (1837), Florida (1845), and Texas (1845) were admitted into the Union, the number of stars thus reaching twenty-eight.

At Beginning of the War between the States

From 1846 until the beginning of the War between the States in 1861, six more states—Iowa (1846), Wisconsin (1848), California (1850), Minnesota (1858), Oregon (1859), and Kansas (1861)—were admitted, and the number of stars increased to thirty-four.

At Beginning of Spanish-American War

From the beginning of the War between the States in 1861 to the commencement of the Spanish-American War in 1898, eleven more states were admitted—West Virginia (1863), Nevada (1864), Nebraska (1867), Colorado (1876), North Dakota (1889), South Dakota (1889), Montana (1889), Washington (1889), Idaho (1890), Wyoming (1890), and Utah (1896)—making the number of stars forty-five.

Today

In 1907 Oklahoma became a state, and in 1912 the territories of New Mexico and Arizona reached their statehood. The stars in the Flag then numbered forty-eight, the number we have today.

In addition to the forty-eight states of the Union, constituting the Continental United States, foreign possessions of such expanse have come under the protection of the Stars and Stripes, as indicated on pages 26–27, that today it may truly be said that the sun never sets on the American Flag.

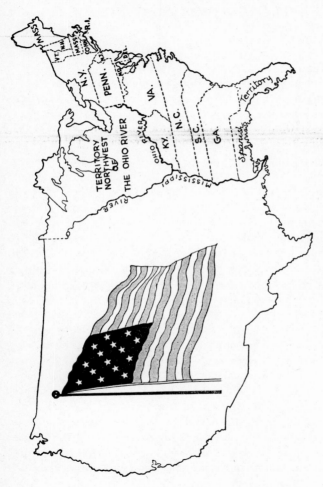

The American Flag from 1795 to 1818

During these twenty-three years the Flag had fifteen stripes.

23

THE BETSY ROSS STORY

The distinction of having made the first American Flag is often given to Betsy Ross, a Quakeress, of Philadelphia. According to the popular story, in June, 1776, shortly before the Declaration of Independence was signed, George Washington, George Ross, and Robert Morris called on Betsy Ross and told her that they, as a Committee of Congress, wanted her to make for them an American flag according to a sketch they had. She replied, "I don't know whether I can, but I'll try." After the Flag was completed, the Committee submitted it to Congress and it was unanimously adopted, thereby giving to Betsy Ross the honor of having made the first American Flag.

Almost without exception, however, historians assail the accuracy of the Betsy Ross Flag story, which is based entirely on family hearsay and is not supported in any way whatsoever by contemporary evidence. To quote the late Admiral George H. Greble, United States Navy, universally acknowledged as America's greatest Flag historian:

"It will probably never be known who designed our union of stars, the records of Congress being silent on the subject, and there being no mention or suggestion of it in any of the voluminous correspondence or diaries of the time, public or private, which have ever been published."

Like the George Washington cherry-tree legend, the Betsy Ross Flag story is intriguing. It appeals to sentiment and satisfies the imagination. We all wish it could be proved to be true. But it is misleading to teach it to American youth as history. It should be taught them as a legend— a tradition. Historically, the question of who made the first American Flag is still unanswered.

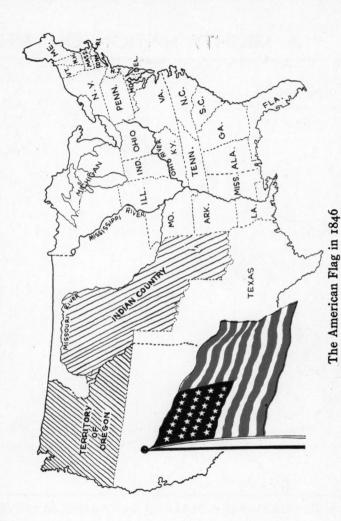

The American Flag in 1846

At the beginning of the Mexican War the Flag had twenty-eight stars.

GREENLAND

CANADA

U. S.

Shaded area represents territory that comprised the Thirteen Original States.

MEXICO

PUERTO RICO

VIRGIN IS.

PANAMA CANAL ZONE

SOUTH AMERICA

DER OUR AMERICAN SYSTEM OF GOVERNMENT

Raising the United States Flag in New Orleans, 1803

TERRITORIAL EXPANSION OF THE UNITED STATES

When the United States was born, July 4, 1776, it was but a strip along the Atlantic seaboard, with an area of about 850,000 square miles. As pioneers wended westward, more territory was acquired and more states were added to the Union; also, other territory came under the protection of the American Flag, until today the Stars and Stripes proudly waves over a great domain of almost 4,000,000 square miles. The following summary shows how the domain was acquired:

Continental United States (3,026,789 sq. miles). Acquired by the release of territory from Great Britain as a result of the War of the Revolution (*territory of the original thirteen states*); by purchase from France (*Louisiana Purchase, 1803*), Spain (*Florida Purchase, 1819*), Mexico (*Gadsden Purchase, 1853*); by accession from the Republic of Texas (admission of Texas as a state, 1845); by cession from Mexico after the Mexican War (more than half a million square miles in the southwest, 1848); and by discovery and exploration.

Puerto Rico (3,435 sq. miles). Ceded by Spain in 1898 by treaty of peace terminating the Spanish-American War.

Virgin Islands (former Danish West Indies—133 sq. miles). Purchased from Denmark in 1917 for $25,000,000. They comprise the islands of St. Thomas, St. John, Saint Croix, and the adjacent islets.

Panama Canal Zone (554 sq. miles). A strip of land five miles in width on each side of the Canal. Perpetual right of occupation was acquired from the Republic of Panama by treaty, February 25, 1904, in consideration of $10,000,000 and the payment of $250,000 a year as long as the United States occupies the Zone.

Alaska (586,400 sq. miles, including the Aleutian Islands—more than twice the size of Texas). Purchased from Russia in 1867 for $7,200,000. It was made a Territory of the Union, August 24, 1912.

Hawaiian Islands (6,407 sq. miles). Annexed in 1898 by the voluntary action of its citizens, the Hawaiian national debt of $4,000,000 being assumed by the United States. The Islands were made a Territory of the Union, June 14, 1900.

Palmyra Island. Although far to the south of the Hawaiian Islands, Palmyra Island, occupying an area about 6 miles long and 1½ miles wide, belongs to the Hawaiian group.

Wake Island (3½ sq. miles). Possession on behalf of the United States was taken January 17, 1899, by the commander of the U.S.S. "Bennington."

American Samoa (Tutuila Island, the largest of the Samoan Islands, and three other islands, with a total area of 75 sq. miles). Acquired in 1899 by arrangement with Great Britain and Germany.

Guam (206 sq. miles). Ceded by Spain in 1898 by treaty of peace terminating the Spanish-American War.

Philippine Islands (114,400 sq. miles, comprising more than 7,000 islands). Ceded by Spain in 1898 by treaty of peace terminating the Spanish-American War. The United States paid Spain $20,000,000 for the Islands.

Howland, Baker, and Jarvis Islands (1 sq. mile, each) are claimed by the United States by reason of discovery during the last century.

IMPORTANT FLAG ANNIVERSARIES

January 1. The Grand Union Flag, the first flag of the United Colonies, was displayed for the first time at Washington's headquarters, Cambridge, Massachusetts, January 1, 1776.

January 26. The United States frigate "Essex" was the first warship to fly the American Flag in the Pacific, January 26, 1813.

January 28. The first display of the American Flag in an attack against a foreign stronghold was at Nassau, Bahama Islands, when, on January 28, 1778, the Americans captured Fort Nassau from the British and raised the Stars and Stripes.

February 14. The first foreign salute to the Stars and Stripes was rendered February 14, 1778, when John Paul Jones, in command of the U.S.S. "Ranger," entered Quiberon Bay, near Brest, France, and received a salute of nine guns.

April 6. Admiral Robert E. Peary, on April 6, 1909, planted the American Flag at the North Pole.

June 14. The First Flag of the United States was adopted by Congress, June 14, 1777.

August 3. The first display of the Stars and Stripes by the Continental Army took place when the Flag was hoisted over Fort Stanwix, New York (the present site of Rome) during the attack by the British, August 3, 1777.

October 17. The American Flag was first saluted by the British at the surrender of Burgoyne's army, October 17, 1777.

October 18. The American Flag was first officially displayed over Alaska at Sitka, October 18, 1867.

THE STAR-SPANGLED BANNER*

O say, can you see by the dawn's early light
  What so proudly we hail'd at the twilight's last gleaming,
Whose broad stripes and bright stars, through the perilous
    fight,
  O'er the ramparts we watch'd, were so gallantly streaming?
    And the rocket's red glare, the bombs bursting in air,
    Gave proof through the night that our flag was still there.
  O say, does that star-spangled banner yet wave
  O'er the land of the free and the home of the brave?

On the shore dimly seen through the mists of the deep,
  Where the foe's haughty host in dread silence reposes,
What is that which the breeze, o'er the towering steep,
  As it fitfully blows, half conceals, half discloses?
    Now it catches the gleam of the morning's first beam,
    In full glory reflected now shines on the stream.
  'Tis the star-spangled banner—O long may it wave
  O'er the land of the free and the home of the brave.

O thus be it e'er when freemen shall stand
  Between their lov'd home and the war's desolation!
Blest with vict'ry and peace may the heav'n rescued land
  Praise the Pow'r that hath made and preserved us a nation!
    Then conquer we must when our cause it is just,
    And this be our motto—"In God is our trust."
  And the star-spangled banner in triumph shall wave
  O'er the land of the free and the home of the brave.

—FRANCIS SCOTT KEY

*The National Education Association in 1912 recommended the above
version as the authorized version of "The Star-Spangled Banner." In
1931 Congress enacted a law making the song our national anthem.

BIRTH OF OUR NATIONAL ANTHEM

No anthem ever written has a more historic, inspiring, and patriotic setting than "The Star-Spangled Banner," which was composed in 1814 when the United States and England were at war. After the British redcoats had burned Washington, the enemy moved on Baltimore, where the soldiers were to attack by land while a powerful British fleet formed for action off Fort McHenry, at the water gates of the city. All during the night of September 13–14, the entire fleet concentrated its fire on the Fort, from whose flagpole flew the Star-Spangled Banner.

Francis Scott Key, from the District of Columbia, was held as a captive on one of the British warships. As the battle raged throughout the night, in silence and darkness he paced the deck of the ship, wondering whether the Flag he had seen when the fight began was still flying over the Fort. It was for him a harrowing night.

At last came the break of day. With strained, eager eyes, through the early morning mist, he saw that the Flag was still there. In patriotic exultation Francis Scott Key, writing on an envelope he had found in his pocket, poured out of his soul the inspiring words of "The Star-Spangled Banner," which later were set to music. Thus the song went forth to sing itself into the hearts of the living generation and of generations to come.

A SONG FOR FLAG DAY*

Your flag and my flag,
    And how it flies to-day
In your land and my land
    And half a world away!
Rose-red and blood-red
    The stripes for ever gleam;
Snow-white and soul-white—
    The good forefathers' dream;

Sky-blue and true blue, with stars to gleam aright—
The gloried guidon of the day; a shelter through the night.

    Your flag and my flag!
    And, oh, how much it holds—

*From *The Trail to Boyland*, by Wilbur D. Nesbit, copyright 1904, 1932. Used by special permission of the publishers, The Bobbs-Merrill Company.

Your land and my land—
  Secure within its folds!
Your heart and my heart
  Beat quicker at the sight;
Sun-kissed and wind-tossed—
  Red and blue and white.

The one flag—the great flag—the flag for me and you—
Glorified all else beside—the red and white and blue!

Your flag and my flag!
  To every star and stripe
The drums beat as hearts beat
  And fifers shrilly pipe!
Your flag and my flag—
  A blessing in the sky;
Your hope and my hope—
  It never hid a lie!

Home land and far land and half the world around,
Old Glory hears our glad salute and ripples to the sound!
                                        —Wilbur D. Nesbit

────────

THE FLAG GOES BY*

Hats off!
Along the street there comes
A blare of bugles, a ruffle of drums,
A flash of color beneath the sky:

*Used by permission of A. S. Barnes and Company.

Hats off!
The flag is passing by!
Blue and crimson and white it shines,
Over the steel-tipped, ordered lines.
Hats off!
The colors before us fly;
But more than the flag is passing by.

Sea-fights and land-fights, grim and great,
Fought to make and to save the State:
Weary marches and sinking ships;
Cheers of victory on dying lips;

Days of plenty and years of peace;
March of a strong land's swift increase;
Equal justice, right, and law,
Stately honor and reverend awe;

Sign of a nation, great and strong
To ward her people from foreign wrong:
Pride and glory and honor—all
Live in the colors to stand or fall.

Hats off!
Along the street there comes
A blare of bugles, a ruffle of drums,
And loyal hearts are beating high:
Hats off!
The flag is passing by!

—HENRY HOLCOMB BENNETT

THE STORY OF "OLD GLORY"

A century or so ago—on March 17, 1824—in Salem, Massachusetts, upon the occasion of the celebration of his twenty-first birthday, William Driver was presented by his mother and a group of Salem girls with a beautiful American Flag.

"I name her 'Old Glory,' " said he, in response to the greetings of the givers, and thus it was that the name "Old Glory" made its advent into the history of our Flag. William Driver's heart and soul were in his occupation of sailing the seas, and from that day on, "Old Glory" accompanied William Driver whenever he went to sea. When, in 1837, after many notable voyages Captain Driver quit the sea and settled in Nashville, Tennessee, "Old Glory" as usual accompanied him. On historic occasions it could be seen gracefully waving from a rope extending from the Captain's house to a tree across the street.

One day, not long before his death, the old Captain placed in the arms of his daughter a bundle, saying:

"Mary Jane, this is my old ship flag, 'Old Glory.' It has been my constant companion on many voyages. I love it as a mother loves her child; take it and cherish it as I have cherished it, for it has been my steadfast friend and protector in all parts of the world, among savages, heathen, and civilized. Keep it always."

"Old Glory" was kept and guarded as a precious heirloom in the Driver family until 1922, when it was sent to the Smithsonian Institution in Washington where it is today, carefully preserved under glass. Every year it is seen by thousands of loyal Americans who visit the capital of their country.

FLAG DAY

June 14, the anniversary of the adoption of the Flag of the United States in 1777, is now quite generally observed as Flag Day.

There are many persons who, in all sincerity, claim the credit of having originated Flag Day. Some of these claimants did do commendable and serious initiative work *locally*, and were honest in their belief that they had originated Flag Day, but they were in ignorance of the fact that patriotic individuals and organizations in other parts of the United States had started similar work years earlier.

June 14 was definitely established as Flag Day by a Proclamation of President Wilson, issued May 30, 1916, in which he said, in part:

"It has, therefore, seemed to me fitting that I should call your attention to the approach of the anniversary of the day upon which the Flag of the United States was adopted by the Congress as the emblem of the Union, and to suggest to you that it should this year and in the years to come be given special significance. . . .

"I therefore suggest and request that throughout the nation, and, if possible, in every community, the fourteenth day of June be observed as FLAG DAY, with special patriotic exercises, at which means shall be taken to give significant expression to our thoughtful love of America . . . our determination to make it greater and purer . . . ."

The above Proclamation of President Wilson was the culmination of a quarter of a century of separate and unconnected efforts by individuals and organizations in different parts of the country in the interest of the observance of June 14 as Flag Day.

HOW TO DISPLAY THE FLAG

On June 14, 1923, a National Flag Conference, attended by representatives from the Army, the Navy, and the principal patriotic, civic, and educational organizations of the country, was held in Washington for the purpose of adopting a Flag Code prescribing correct ways of displaying and respecting the Flag of the United States. In addressing the opening session of the Conference, President Harding said:

"Everything we do to bring the Flag into proper consideration by the citizenship of the Republic is highly commendable and deserves to be cordially indorsed.

"Every salutation to the Flag makes my consecration to the Country and the Flag a little more secure."

The rules for Flag display that follow are based on the Code that was adopted by the National Flag Conference. They are the National Flag Code annotated and illustrated.

GENERAL RULES

The Flag should be displayed from sunrise to sunset on buildings and on stationary flag staffs in the open.

Unless there is some special reason for doing so, the Flag should not be flown in rainy or stormy weather.

The Flag should always be raised briskly and lowered slowly and ceremoniously.

When the Flag is being raised or lowered, it must never be allowed to touch the ground.

In a procession with another flag:

The United States Flag is on the marching right.

In a procession with a line of other flags:

The United States Flag is in front of the center of the line.

When displayed either vertically or horizontally against a wall, in a show window, or elsewhere:

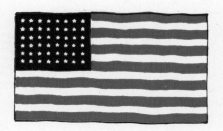

The blue field is uppermost and to the Flag's own right—that is, to the observer's left.

When used on a speaker's platform:

(*a*) *If displayed flat, the Flag is above and behind the speaker.*
(*b*) *If flown from a staff, the Flag is in the position of honor, at the speaker's right, and preferably slightly in front.*

Note

If the speaker should not be on a platform but on the floor, on the same level with the audience, the Flag of the United States, if flown from a staff, would be at the speaker's right, and preferably slightly in front.

When displayed from a staff projecting horizontally or at an angle from the window sill, balcony, or front of a building:

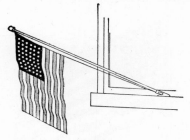

The blue field of the Flag goes clear to the peak.

When displayed with another flag against a wall, staffs crossed:

The United States Flag is on the observer's left, and its staff is in front of the staff of the other flag.

When flown on the same halyard with flags of states or cities, or pennants of societies:

The United States Flag is at the peak.

NOTES

1. In the Army there is no exception to this rule. In the Navy, however, the church pennant—which, by the way, is not the flag of the church but a signal flag to indicate that the crew is at church—is flown above the National Flag during divine service on shipboard, according to Navy custom. But this pennant represents no particular church. It merely signifies that divine service is being conducted.

2. It is considered better form never to fly any other flag on the same staff with the Flag of the United States, but instead to fly the other flag on another staff.

When the United States Flag and flags of other nations, states, or cities, or pennants of societies, are flown from adjacent staffs:

*The United States Flag is on the right of the line—
that is, on the observer's left.*

NOTES

1. When the United States Flag and flags of other nations, states, or cities, or pennants of societies, are flown from adjacent staffs, the United States Flag is hoisted first and lowered last.

2. When the United States Flag is flown with flags of other nations, all staffs should be of the same height and the flags of approximately equal size.

3. International usage forbids the display of the flag of any one nation above that of any other nation in time of peace.

In a group of flags of states or cities, or pennants of societies, displayed from staffs:

(3) (1) (2) (4)

The United States Flag is at the center or at the highest point of the group.

NOTE

In a group of flags of different nations, an arrangement to which no one could take exception would be to place the flags alphabetically, alternately on the right and on the left of the United States Flag. For example, in the case of France, Germany, Great Britain, and Japan, the flag of France would occupy the position (1), Germany (2), Great Britain (3), and Japan (4).

When suspended over a sidewalk from a rope, extending
from a house to a pole at the edge of the sidewalk:

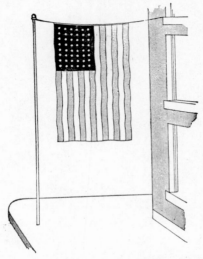

*The Flag is hoisted a part of the way out from the
building, toward the pole, blue field first.*

On a float in a parade:

The Flag is displayed from a staff.

When displayed over the middle of a street:

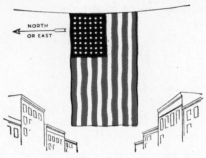

The Flag is suspended vertically, with the blue field to the north in an east-and-west street, or to the east in a north-and-south street.

When displayed on an automobile:

The Flag may be fastened to the body, or clamped to the radiator cap, as shown above.

NOTE

Under no circumstances should the Flag ever be draped over the hood, top, or sides of an automobile.

When displayed in a church:

If in the chancel, the United States Flag is in the position of honor at the clergyman's right as he faces the audience, and the church or other flag is at his left.

If outside the chancel, the United States Flag is in the position of honor at the right of the congregation as it faces the clergyman, and the state or other flag is at its left.

Note

This rule for the display of the Flag in a church applies to any other building or hall.

To indicate mourning when the Flag is flown from a stationary staff:

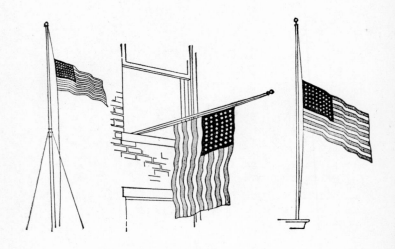

The Flag is placed at half-staff.

NOTES

1. The position of half-staff, or half-mast, is considered to be some distance (not necessarily halfway down) from the top of the staff.

2. When the Flag is to be flown at half-staff, it should be hoisted to the peak for an instant and then lowered to the half-staff. Before being lowered for the day, the Flag should be raised to the peak.

**To indicate mourning when the Flag is fastened to a small
staff, as when carried in a parade:**

*Two streamers of black crepe of suitable length are attached
to the spearhead, and allowed to fall naturally.*

When used to cover a casket:

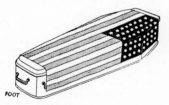

*The union of the Flag is at the head of the casket and over the
left shoulder of the deceased.*

NOTES

1. The casket should be carried foot first.
    2. The Flag must not be lowered into the grave, or allowed
to touch the ground.

CAUTIONS TO OBSERVE IN DISPLAY

1. Do not permit disrespect to be shown to the Flag of the United States.

2. Do not dip the Flag to any person or any thing. The regimental color or state, organization, or institutional flag will render this honor.

3. Do not display the Flag with the union down except as a signal of distress.

4. Do not place any other flag or pennant above or to the right of the Flag of the United States.*

5. Do not place any object or emblem of any kind on or above the Flag of the United States.

6. Do not use the Flag as drapery in any form whatsoever. Use bunting of red, white, and blue.

7. Do not drape the Flag over the hood, top, sides, or back of a vehicle, or of a railway train or boat.

8. Do not use the Flag as a covering for a ceiling.

9. Do not carry the Flag flat or horizontally, but always aloft and free.

10. Do not let the Flag touch the ground or the floor, or trail in the water.

11. Do not use the Flag as a portion of a costume or of an athletic uniform. Do not embroider it upon cushions or handkerchiefs or print it on paper napkins or boxes.

12. Do not put lettering of any kind upon the Flag.

13. Do not use the Flag in any form of advertising or fasten an advertising sign to a pole from which the Flag is flown.

14. Do not display, use, or store the Flag in such a manner as will permit it to be easily soiled or damaged.

* See Note 1, page 44, for the only exception to this caution.

FLAG NEVER TO BE DRAPED

The Flag of the United States is an artistic, well-proportioned emblem whose beauty should not be marred by draping. Draping may be done with red, white, and blue bunting, but not with the Flag.

Bunting of the national colors should be used over the front of a platform and for decoration in general. The bunting must always be arranged with the blue on top, or to the observer's left, white in the middle, and red below or to the observer's right. *The reason for this is that the blue, being the color of the union of the Flag, is the "honor color," and should therefore come first, either horizontally or vertically.*

DESTRUCTION OF UNSIGHTLY FLAGS

Torn, soiled, or badly faded Flags should not be displayed. When a Flag is in such a condition that it is no longer a fitting emblem to display, it should be destroyed as a whole, privately, preferably by burning or by some other method lacking in any suggestion of irreverence or disrespect.

WHEN TO DISPLAY THE FLAG

The Flag should be displayed on all National and State Holidays, and on historic and special occasions, as follows:

January 20 (1941, etc., every fourth year thereafter). On the day the President of the United States is inaugurated.

February 12. Lincoln's Birthday.

February 22. Washington's Birthday.

April 6. Army Day. (Anniversary of the entrance of the United States into the World War, April 6, 1917.)

Second Sunday in May. Mother's Day.

May 30. Memorial Day. The Flag to be at half-staff until noon, and at full staff from noon to sunset.

June 14. Flag Day.

July 4. Independence Day.

First Monday in September. Labor Day.

September 14. Anniversary of the writing of "The Star-Spangled Banner" by Francis Scott Key.

September 17. Constitution Day. (Anniversary of the adoption of the Constitution of the United States, September 17, 1787.)

Last Sunday in September. Gold Star Mother's Day.

October 12. Columbus Day.

October 27. Navy Day. (Anniversary of the birth of President Theodore Roosevelt.)

The first Tuesday after the first Monday in November in 1940, etc., every fourth year. Presidential election.

November 11. Armistice Day.

Last Thursday in November. Thanksgiving Day.

In the various states the Flag should be displayed on **Admission Day** and all **Election Days.**

SALUTING THE FLAG

During the ceremony of hoisting or lowering the Flag, or when the Flag is passing in a parade, everyone present should face the Flag, stand at attention, and salute.

Those in uniform should render the hand salute. When not in uniform, men should remove the headdress with the right hand and hold it at the left shoulder, the hand being over the heart. In case of inclement weather the hat may be slightly raised and held above the head. Men without hats merely stand at attention, without saluting, unless they belong to the naval or military service.

Women should salute the Flag by placing the right hand over the heart.

If the Flag is passing by, the salute is rendered when the Flag is five or six paces away and is held until it has passed.

SALUTE TO THE NATIONAL ANTHEM

When "The Star-Spangled Banner" is played, everyone present should stand at attention and salute as described above. The salute is rendered at the first note of the anthem, and the position is retained until the last note.

PLEDGE TO THE FLAG

In pledging allegiance to the Flag of the United States, the approved practice in schools, which is suitable for civilian adults, is as follows:

Fig. 1   Fig. 2

Standing, with the right hand over the heart (Fig. 1), all the pupils repeat together:

I pledge allegiance to the Flag of the United States of America and to the Republic for which it stands, one nation indivisible, with liberty and justice for all.

At the words, "to the Flag," the right hand is extended, palm upward, toward the Flag (Fig. 2), and this position is held to the end. After the words, "justice for all," the hand drops to the side.

However, civilian adults will always show full respect to the Flag, when the pledge is being given, by merely standing at attention, men removing the headdress.

Persons in uniform should render the hand salute.

COAT OF ARMS
OF THE UNITED STATES

The Coat of Arms of the United States consists of an eagle with wings and feet outspread and bearing the following distinguishing devices:

Shield. On the eagle's breast is the *Shield of the United States*, consisting of thirteen vertical stripes, symbolizing the thirteen original states. The blue upper part of the shield is called the *chief.*

Crest. The crest over the head of the eagle shows thirteen stars breaking through a cloud, denoting a new constellation in the firmament of sovereign powers.

E pluribus unum. This Latin phrase, "One out of Many," alludes to the one Union formed out of many states.

Olive branch and arrows. The olive branch and the arrows (thirteen) in the talons of the eagle denote the power of peace and war which is vested in Congress.

The Coat of Arms of the United States should be used only by those who are authorized by law and custom to do so. Under no circumstances should the Coat of Arms or the Shield of the United States be used for advertising purposes.

FLAG LAWS

Legislation to prevent misuse, abuse, or desecration of the Flag of the United States is left to the states of the Union for their respective jurisdictions and to the federal government for the District of Columbia. Neither Congress nor any of the states has enacted any laws regarding the manner of displaying or saluting the Flag.

FEDERAL FLAG LAWS

With the exception of the law of June 14, 1777, adopting the Flag, and of subsequent laws affecting the design of the Flag, Congress has so far passed only five laws regarding the Flag:

1. *Trademarks.* The Act of Congress of February 20, 1905, provides that a trademark cannot be registered which consists of, or comprises among other things, "the Flag, coat of arms, or other insignia of the United States, or any simulation thereof."

2. *Mother's Day.* A joint resolution of Congress, approved May 8, 1914, enjoins the display of the Flag on Mother's Day.

3. *Prevention of desecration in District of Columbia.* The Act of February 8, 1917, provides certain penalties for the desecration, mutilation, or improper use of the Flag within the District of Columbia.

4. *Dismissal from government service.* The Act of May 16, 1918, provides for the dismissal from the service, when the United States is at war, of any employee or official of the United States government who criticizes in an abusive or violent manner the Flag of the United States.

5. *Gold Star Mother's Day.* A joint resolution of Con-

gress, approved June 23, 1936, enjoins the display of the Flag on Gold Star Mother's Day (the last Sunday in September).

STATE FLAG LAWS

Every state in the Union has a law prohibiting the abuse, misuse, or desecration of the Flag of the United States. In most cases the provisions of the law cover also the abuse, misuse, or desecration of the state flag; also, in many cases, the misuse or desecration of the national and of the state shields and coats of arms.

The purpose of these laws is to prevent and punish: (*a*) the placing of any word, figure, mark, picture, design, drawing, or advertisement of whatever nature upon the Flag of the United States, or upon any picture or other representation of the Flag of the United States; and (*b*) the mutilation, defacement, defiance, abuse, or improper use of the Flag, including the use of the Flag for the purpose of advertising the sale of merchandise.

FLAG OF UNITED STATES DEFINED

According to the Flag laws of the District of Columbia and nearly all the states, the words "Flag of the United States" include any flag, or any picture of any flag, in which the colors, the stars, and the stripes may be shown in any number which, without careful examination or deliberation, the average person may believe to represent the Flag of the United States.

EVERY
STAR
A STATE
—
EVERY
STATE
A STAR

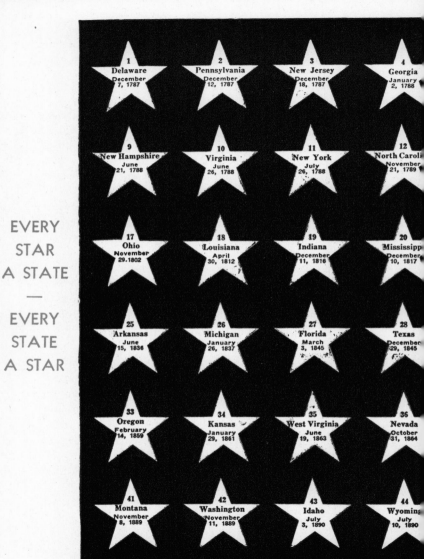

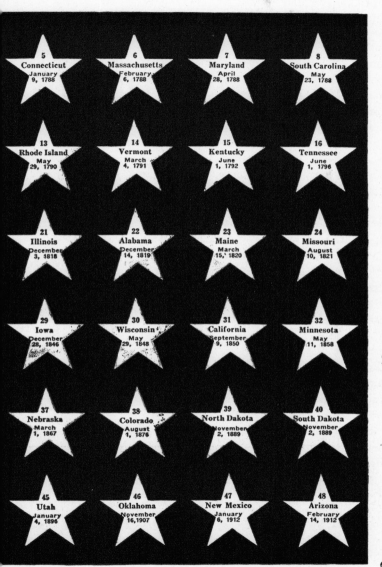

5 Connecticut January 9, 1788	**6** Massachusetts February 6, 1788	**7** Maryland April 28, 1788	**8** South Carolina May 23, 1788
13 Rhode Island May 29, 1790	**14** Vermont March 4, 1791	**15** Kentucky June 1, 1792	**16** Tennessee June 1, 1796
21 Illinois December 3, 1818	**22** Alabama December 14, 1819	**23** Maine March 15, 1820	**24** Missouri August 10, 1821
29 Iowa December 28, 1846	**30** Wisconsin May 29, 1848	**31** California September 9, 1850	**32** Minnesota May 11, 1858
37 Nebraska March 1, 1867	**38** Colorado August 1, 1876	**39** North Dakota November 2, 1889	**40** South Dakota November 2, 1889
45 Utah January 4, 1896	**46** Oklahoma November 16, 1907	**47** New Mexico January 6, 1912	**48** Arizona February 14, 1912

Pick
Out
the
Star
of
Your
State

GLOSSARY OF FLAG TERMS

canton: a rectangular division of a flag or ensign, usually in the upper corner next to the staff and containing the national or other device

color: in the military service, the national flag carried by unmounted units. The expression, "The Colors," is used quite generally in referring to a flag

dip: to lower a flag as a salute

ensign: in the Navy, the term for the national flag

field: the ground of each division in a flag

fly: the side of a flag extending from the staff to the flying end—that is, the long side

half-mast: to lower a flag some distance (not necessarily halfway down) from the top of the staff, as a token of mourning

halyard: a rope or cord with which a flag is drawn to the top of the staff, and with which it is lowered

hoist: the side of a flag extending along the staff—that is, the short side. To *hoist* a flag is to raise it to the top of the staff

increscent: the new moon depicted with the points turned toward the dexter (right) side

standard: the national flag carried in the military service by mounted or motorized units

strike: to haul a flag down in token of surrender

union: a design emblematic of union, used on a national flag or ensign, sometimes covering the whole field, sometimes occupying an upper inner corner. The union of the Flag of the United States is the cluster of forty-eight stars on the field of blue, symbolizing the union of the states

THE INDEX

90 up